FRUITS

Are Good For You!

by
Gloria Koster

PEBBLE
a capstone imprint

Published by Pebble, an imprint of Capstone
1710 Roe Crest Drive
North Mankato, Minnesota 56003
capstonepub.com

Library of Congress Cataloging-in-Publication Data
Names: Koster, Gloria, author.
Title: Fruits are good for you! / by Gloria Koster.
Description: North Mankato, Minnesota : Pebble, [2023] | Series: Healthy foods | Includes bibliographical references and index. | Audience: Ages 5-8 | Audience: Grades K-1 | Summary: "Blueberries, oranges, and avocados . . . They're all part of the fruits group, and they're all healthy foods! Discover where fruits come from, what nutrition they provide, and how they help form a healthy diet. Jampacked with fun facts and full-color photos, this Pebble Explore book is perfect for curious young readers and report writers alike"-- Provided by publisher.
Identifiers: LCCN 2022008201 (print) | LCCN 2022008202 (ebook) |
    ISBN 9781666351255 (hardcover) | ISBN 9781666351316 (paperback) |
    ISBN 9781666351378 (pdf) | ISBN 9781666351491 (kindle edition)
Subjects: LCSH: Fruit in human nutrition--Juvenile literature.
Classification: LCC QP144.F78 K67 2023 (print) | LCC QP144.F78 (ebook) | DDC 613.2--dc23/eng/20220602
LC record available at https://lccn.loc.gov/2022008201
LC ebook record available at https://lccn.loc.gov/2022008202

Editorial Credits
Editor: Donald Lemke; Designer: Tracy Davies; Media Researcher: Julie De Adder; Production Specialist: Katy LaVigne

Image Credits
Getty Images: Don Mason, 15, Inti St Clair, 25, Jose Luis Pelaez Inc, 4, Terry Vine, 9; Shutterstock: Alexei Logvinovich, 28, all_about_people, 12, Anna Kucherova, 8, apiguide, 26, Arimag, 18, Astarina (doodles), cover and throughout, Dmitri Belokoni, 7, GolfX, cover (front), hanapon1002, 19, Iraida Bearlala (background), cover and throughout, Jenson, 23, Lorraine Hudgins, 21, lovelypeace, 27, Mauro Rodrigues, 5, patjo, 16, Pixel-Shot, 29, pullia, 6, soumen82hazra, 14, Tatiana Gladskikh, 17, VCoscaron, 13, wavebreakmedia, 22; USDA: 11

TABLE OF CONTENTS

Words in **bold** are defined in the glossary.

WHAT ARE FRUITS?

Add strawberries and blueberries to a bowl. Slice apples and put them in too. Then add grapes and melon. You made a fruit salad!

Oranges grow on trees.

These healthy foods belong to the fruits group.

Fruits come from trees and other plants. Some grow in the wild. Others are planted by farmers.

All fruits have seeds inside.

Some fruits have a lot. Others have one seed called a pit. Peaches and plums have pits.

Apples have several seeds inside.

Fruits have many kinds of skin. The skin can be soft or hard. It can be smooth like a banana peel. It can even be spiky like the outside of a pineapple.

Some foods people think are vegetables are really fruits. Most people think tomatoes are veggies. Tomatoes have seeds. They are fruits! Cucumbers are fruits too.

Many people eat avocados. They use them to make **guacamole** for tacos and chips. Avocados are fruits!

Guacamole includes both avocados and tomatoes.

EATING FRUITS IS IMPORTANT

MyPlate is a guide for healthy meals. Half your plate should have grains and **protein** foods. The other half should have vegetables and fruits.

Most fruits taste sweet but can still be healthy. They have a type of sugar called **fructose**. This sugar gives you energy.

Think of a car. It needs fuel to keep going. Fruits give your body a burst of fuel. The fuel helps you stay active.

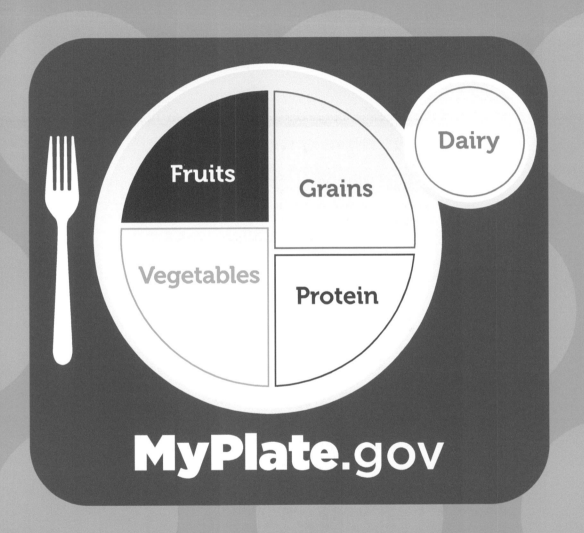

Fruits have **vitamins** and minerals to keep you healthy. **Citrus** fruits contain vitamin C. Eat them for strong teeth and gums.

Bananas have a mineral called **potassium**. It is good for your nerves and muscles.

Orange fruits get their color from **beta-carotene**. Your body changes beta-carotene into vitamin A. This vitamin is good for your skin. It can also keep you from getting sick.

Fruits contain a lot of water too.
Your body needs water to do its jobs.
Every bit helps!

Watermelon has more water than nearly any other fruit.

HOW FRUITS GROW

Different fruits grow in different ways. Some grow on trees or on bushes. Other fruits grow on vines or the ground.

Cherries grow on trees.

Fruit plants need sun and water. They also need a gas called **carbon dioxide** to help them grow. The plants make flowers. Soon the flowers turn into fruits.

Many people like to pick fruits. Visit a grove to pick oranges or lemons. Head to an orchard for apples or pears.

Have you seen a bush with berries? First, ask an adult if they are safe to eat. Then take some home in a basket.

Green fruits may not be ready to eat. Wait until they are ripe. Animals like the bright colors of ripe fruits too.

Birds also eat fruit seeds. When they do, some seeds drop onto the ground. These seeds make new plants.

Many birds eat berries from trees.

SMART CHOICES

How much fruit do you need? That depends on your age and size. It also depends on how much you move.

Most people need one or two cups of fruit every day. You can eat a whole fruit like an apple. Or drink fruit juice, like orange or apple juice.

Whole fruits are healthier because they have **fiber**. Fiber makes you feel full. It is good for **digestion** too.

Go shopping with a grown-up. Try to buy fruits that are fresh. You can buy local fruits at a fruit stand. Supermarkets sell fresh fruits too.

You can also buy canned, frozen, or dried fruits. Be sure to read food labels. Avoid items with extra sugar added.

Fruits are low in fat and salt. Snacking on a piece of fruit helps keep you from eating foods that are not as healthy.

Dragon fruit are common in South America.

Check out new types of fruits! Have you tasted dragon fruit? This fruit grows on cactus plants. What about an African cucumber? It is spiky on the outside and tastes sour on the inside.

Try a star fruit. This fruit is popular in Asia. Or test out some jackfruit. Some people cook this fruit like meat.

Star fruit are shaped like stars.

Be creative! Fruits go well with other healthy foods. Spread some nut butter on apple slices. Add fruit to yogurt or smoothies. Put fruit on top of your pancakes.

With fruits and exercise, you'll stay healthy and strong!

GLOSSARY

beta-carotene (BAY-tuh KAYR-uh-teen)—a natural substance found in orange, yellow, and dark green fruits and vegetables that helps your body grow and be healthy

carbon dioxide (KAR-buhn dye-OK-side)—a gas that is a mix of carbon and oxygen; people and animals breath out this gas and plants absorb it

citrus (SIT-ruhss)—a kind of tree that produces acidic, juicy fruit, such as an orange, a lemon, or a grapefruit

digestion (duh-JESS-chuhn)—the process of breaking down foods in the stomach and organs so it can be used in the body

fiber (FYE-bur)—a part of foods, such as fruits and vegetables, that helps foods move through the intestines

fructose (FROOK-tohs)—a very sweet kind of sugar that is found in fruit juices and honey

guacamole (gwah-kuh-MOH-lee)—a dip made from avocado, tomotoes, onions, and seasonings

potassium (puh-TASS-ee-uhm)—a silvery-white mineral found in some foods, including bananas

protein (PRO-teen)—one type of nutrient found in food

vitamins (VI-tuh-minz)—nutrients in food that work along with minerals to keep us healthy

READ MORE

Schuh, Mari. *Food Is Fuel*. North Mankato, MN: Capstone, 2021.

Schwartz, Heather E. *Cookie Monster's Foodie Truck: A Sesame Street Celebration of Food*. Minneapolis: Lerner Publications, 2020.

Webster, Christy. *Follow That Food!* New York: Random House, 2021.

INTERNET SITES

Harvard School of Public Health: "The Nutrition Source"
hsph.harvard.edu/nutritionsource/what-should-you-eat/vegetables-and-fruits

Healthy Kids Association: "Fruit"
healthy-kids.com.au/food-nutrition/5-food-groups/fruit

USDA MyPlate: "Fruits"
myplate.gov/search?keyword=fruit

INDEX

ABOUT THE AUTHOR

A public and school librarian, Gloria Koster belongs to the Children's Book Committee of Bank Street College of Education. She enjoys both city and country life, dividing her time between Manhattan and the small town of Pound Ridge, New York. Gloria has three adult children and a bunch of energetic grandkids.